Foreword by Colin Buchanan

Jesus, Strong and Kind

Written by
Sinclair B. Ferguson

Illustrated by
Angelo Ruta

CF4•K

A Big Thank-You

to Rich Thompson, Jonny Robinson,
Michael Farren and Colin Buchanan for
composing *Jesus, Strong and Kind* and
letting us all sing it.

This book belongs to

_____

10 9 8 7 6 5 4 3 2 1

Copyright © 2024 Sinclair B. Ferguson

ISBN: 978-1-5271-1000-7

Published by Christian Focus Publications,

Geanies House, Fearn, Tain, Ross-shire, IV20 1TW, U.K.

Illustrations by Angelo Ruta
Design by Pete Barnsley (CreativeHoot.com)

Printed and bound in Malaysia

The song *Jesus Strong and Kind* was written by: Rich Thompson, Jonny Robinson, Michael Farren, Colin Buchanan.

CCLI Song # 7139992 © 2019 CityAlight Music | Wanaaring Road Music. All rights reserved. www.ccli.com

Unless otherwise indicated, Scripture quotations are from The Holy Bible, English Standard Version, published by HarperCollins Publishers copyright © 2001 by Crossway Bibles, a division of Good News Publishers. Used by permission. All rights reserved.

Contents

Jesus,

Jesus said that if I thirst,
I should come to Him.
No one else can satisfy,
I should come to Him.

For the Lord is good and faithful.
He will keep us day and night.
We can always run to Jesus.
Jesus, strong and kind.

Jesus said, if I am weak,
I should come to Him.
No one else can be my strength,
I should come to Him.

For the Lord is good and faithful.
He will keep us day and night.
We can always run to Jesus.
Jesus, strong and kind.

Strong and Kind

Jesus said that if I fear,
I should come to Him.
No one else can be my shield.
I should come to Him.

For the Lord is good and faithful.
He will keep us day and night.
We can always run to Jesus.
Jesus, strong and kind.

Jesus said, if I am lost,
He will come to me.
And He showed me on that cross.
He will come to me.

For the Lord is good and faithful.
He will keep us day and night.
We can always run to Jesus.
Jesus, strong and kind.
Jesus, strong and kind.

Foreword

I recently heard a Bible teacher say, 'If you want to get to know Jesus, go to the Gospels! That's where we really get to know Jesus.'

That Bible teacher was Sinclair Ferguson. When I heard him say that, he wasn't speaking to children. He was speaking to other Bible teachers, grown-ups who had spent years studying and preaching God's Word.

But that's the wonderful thing about getting to know Jesus. Young or old, Jesus says, 'Come to me.'

When I wrote *Jesus, Strong and Kind* with my friends, we wanted to write a song that was simple to sing but that would help everyone who sings it to get to know Jesus. By God's grace, lots of people, big and small, near and far, know and love to sing *Jesus, Strong and Kind*.

And now, my friend Sinclair, invites us all to walk with him into the truths of this little song, into the Gospels, where we'll step into the stories from God's Word that show us the greatness and the goodness of Jesus. I think we might even sing the song together along the way.

Are you ready to get to know Jesus better? Me too!

C'mon, let's go!

Colin Buchanan,
Songwriter, *Jesus, Strong and Kind*

Jesus

I wonder, what do you think about Jesus?

I wonder what your friends would say?

Some of our friends may know almost nothing about Jesus. Perhaps you know people who use the name of the Lord Jesus only as a swear word.

Some people think of Jesus as though he were a policeman. They make the mistake of thinking that if they trust him he'll spoil their lives!

That's so wrong, isn't it? It's sad too.

Perhaps you know about Jesus, but have never really trusted him.

If we are going to trust Jesus, we need to know what he is really like.

The song *Jesus, Strong and Kind* tells us who Jesus is and how much he loves us. It doesn't tell us everything about him, of course. No song could do that. No book could do that!

In fact, the apostle John wrote these words at the end of his Gospel:

Now there are many other things that Jesus did. Were every one of them to be written, I suppose that the world itself could not contain the books that would be written (John 21:25).

John was probably smiling when he wrote that. He realised that the Lord Jesus really is too wonderful to describe fully, but here is something we can be sure of: Jesus is strong and kind.

In this book we are going to think together about him.

Watch CityAlight
featuring
Colin Buchanan
singing *Jesus,*
Strong and Kind

Purchase &
download *Jesus,*
Strong and Kind
resources

Thirst

One day, Jesus said
'. . . Whoever believes in me
shall never thirst.'

John 6:35

In the first verse of *Jesus, Strong and Kind* we sing about that.

Jesus said that if I thirst,
I should come to Him.
No one else can satisfy,
I should come to Him.

For the Lord is good and faithful.
He will keep us day and night.
We can always run to Jesus.
Jesus, strong and kind.

One day Jesus and his disciples were travelling to Galilee where they all lived. Jesus wanted to take a road that went through a country called Samaria.

The disciples were Jews. They must have wondered why Jesus wanted them to go that way. The people who lived in Samaria were not friendly to Jews. And many of the Jews didn't like the Samaritans much either!

Perhaps Jesus wanted to take a short cut? The disciples realised that Jesus knew best, even if they didn't always understand him.

He always does know best.

About lunch time they all arrived at a town called Sychar. They were hot and hungry. They needed food.

Jesus saw a well and told his disciples, 'That's Jacob's Well. You go and get the food. I'm feeling tired, but let's meet there later.'

As the disciples went into the town to buy food for lunch. Jesus sat down beside the well.

That is when something unusual happened.

Jesus looked up and saw someone coming out of the village. They were all on their own.

'That's strange,' Jesus thought. 'What are they doing? It's the middle of the day. The sun's beating down. It's hot. Why would anyone come out of the town at this time of day? There must be a reason.'

When the person came nearer Jesus noticed something else:

'It's a woman! Why is she coming out here in the middle of the day all on her own? Why is nobody with her?

'My heavenly Father always has a purpose in everything that happens to me. Maybe this is why he led me through Samaria. I'll find out why this woman has come here alone in the middle of the day, but I believe I already know!'

The woman was not expecting to see anyone. What a surprise she got to see someone else at Jacob's Well! 'What is this man doing here all on his own? Who

is this stranger? He looks like a Jew, and he doesn't have anything to draw water with from the well!'

When she reached the well, Jesus asked her if she would give him a drink of water.

Jesus created the world and every drop of water in it, but he asked this woman to give him a drink! He could change water into wine. Why didn't he command a glass of water to appear in front of him? Why did he ask this woman to give him a drink? Did he not know she was a difficult sort of person?

Jesus had a good reason. He planned to invite this woman to trust him as her Saviour.

Instead of replying politely to Jesus' request, the woman snapped back at him!

'Who do you think you are? You're a Jew. You hate Samaritans and you don't think much of women either—and I'm both! You ask me for a drink! Huh. Get your own drink!'

What she said was true of some Jews. They didn't like Samaritans and looked down their noses at them. Some Jewish men even treated their wives badly, but Jesus wasn't like that.

Jesus' reply really surprised her, 'If you knew about the gift God wants to give you, and if you knew who was asking you for a drink, you would have asked me for a drink of the water I have! If you had asked me, I would have given you living water.'

What a strange thing to say! What did Jesus mean? The woman didn't know what to think about Jesus, but she was the kind of person who always wanted to have the last word.

'You can give me living water?' she said. 'You don't even have a bucket! How are you going to get water? Are you going to make it spring up from nowhere? Just look at this well. Have you no idea how deep it is?

'If you're planning to give me living water, you're just silly. Do you think you're greater than Jacob who dug this well? Who do you think you are, coming here and talking about giving me living water?'

What a way to speak to the Lord Jesus! How do you think he responded? Well, Jesus is strong, but he's kind too. We can see his strength and his kindness in the patience he showed this woman.

Maybe it's not surprising that she was at the well on her own. Nobody would have wanted to spend time with her. She always seemed to put other people down.

However, Jesus' kind and patient words were far more powerful than hers.

Jesus said to her,

'Listen, you've come here in the hot noon-day sun, to draw water from this famous well. Why do you do that? It's because every day you're thirsty—isn't that true? Everyone who comes here to get water will have to come back again, and again. That's because this kind of water can satisfy your thirst only for a short time.

'Now I can give you a different kind of water to drink, so that you will never be thirsty again. It will be like a spring inside you. This water is water for your soul, and it will give you eternal life!'

Jesus could give this woman life that would last for ever. That's how strong Jesus is! And what's really amazing is that he was willing to give this living water to a woman who was being so unpleasant to him.

That's how kind Jesus is.

Still the woman wanted to have the last word!

'If you've got this water let's see it! Then I can stay at home tomorrow, and I won't need to come out here ever again!'

She didn't really believe what Jesus was saying.

How did Jesus respond to that?

Jesus said something that startled the woman. 'I want you to go back to the village, get your husband, and bring him back here with you to meet me.'

She snapped back, 'I don't have a husband!'

Why did Jesus suddenly start talking about her husband? Isn't that odd?

Not really. You see, Jesus knew something about this woman, something that we still have to discover.

Jesus said to her, 'I know you don't have a husband. You've had five husbands already. More than that: I know that the man you're living with now isn't your husband.'

How did Jesus know all this?

Jesus is the Son of God. He knows everything. That's all we really need to know. But, there is something else . . .

Some people can sense things that aren't obvious to others, can't they? They can tell if someone can't be trusted. Or they can sense if something is troubling another person. Other people don't notice it, but they do. That's difficult to explain; but it's real.

The Lord Jesus was like that. In fact, John tells us (in John 2:24-25), that Jesus 'knew all people . . . he himself knew what was in man.' He didn't have any sin in his life, so I think he must have been able to see right into people's hearts! Perhaps this woman had given him some clues about herself without even knowing it. There was something not quite right about her.

She didn't like the way Jesus could tell her things about herself. She wanted to get away from him and his questions!

Have you ever watched people on TV being asked questions they don't want to answer? What do they do? They change the topic, don't they? They don't answer the question they've been asked. They start talking about something else.

That's exactly what the woman at Jacob's Well did.

'So, you're a prophet, are you?' She said, 'Well then, Mr Prophet, I have a question for you.'

Now she felt she was back in control. Now Jesus was having to answer her questions!

'Answer this question, Mr Prophet! Our forefathers said we should worship here in Samaria. Your teachers say we should worship in Jerusalem. Which is it? What's your view? Who is right?'

We know Jesus is strong and kind, but look how patient he is as well. He told her there was something far more important than her question!

'Where you worship isn't the most important thing. What is important is whether you know God and experience his love and the salvation he promises to give to those who trust him. What really matters now, is worshipping the Father in spirit and truth.'

This means that the most important thing in the world is knowing, trusting, loving, and worshipping God. We do that with the help of the Holy Spirit and by trusting in the Lord Jesus who is the truth.

The woman still had something else to say: 'You're right. I don't know who you are, but when the Messiah comes, he'll explain everything.'

Right from the beginning of the Bible, God had promised that a Saviour would come. In Deuteronomy 18:18-19 he had promised that one day he would raise up a prophet like Moses who would speak God's Word truly. The woman at the well knew that promise.

Imagine how the woman must have felt when Jesus quietly replied, 'I am the Messiah. Yes, I , the person speaking to you, am the Saviour God promised to send. I am the one you have heard about all your life. I am he.'

Those words 'I am he' must have made her think. I AM HE was the name God had revealed to Moses when he met him at the burning bush. She knew that story from the Book of Exodus chapter three.

Could this stranger be the I AM, the Son of God, the Messiah? He had spoken kindly to her, but could he save someone like her, and give her eternal life?

By this time the disciples were coming back with the food they had bought. As they looked through the dust and haze they saw that Jesus was talking to somebody at Jacob's Well. It was the middle of the day—how odd!

Then, as they got nearer, they could see from the clothes the person was wearing that it was a Samaritan woman! What was going on?

Just then, the woman got up, turned round, and ran down the path back to the town—leaving her water bottle behind!

What do you think happened next? Something amazing.

The woman started speaking to everyone she met about Jesus and about what he had said.

'You've got to come quickly. There's a man at Jacob's Well who told me all about myself. I've never seen him in my life before now; but he knows everything about me—all the things you know about me and more! He said he was the promised Messiah. Do you think he can really be the Messiah? You've got to come!'

And they went. Soon many of them came to trust in Jesus for themselves. They discovered that he really was the Messiah, the Saviour. It was just as the woman had said. They even asked him to stay for a few days. Then more people in the town came to trust him.

Here is what they said to the woman: 'Now we believe not just because of what you told us, but because we've met him for ourselves. Now we know that Jesus is the Saviour of the world!'

When the woman ran back into the town to speak to her neighbours, she forgot all about her water jar! She left it there at Jacob's Well. John remembered seeing that. He must have thought it was interesting. The woman had just discovered the water Jesus promised and would never be thirsty again! She forgot all about the water from Jacob's Well!

I love this story about Jesus, don't you? It shows us how kind he is and what a wonderful Saviour he is. This story shows us that when nobody else can help, we can go to Jesus and ask him to be our Saviour, friend and Lord.

If we do, we will discover what the woman at the well discovered. Jesus is strong and kind.

If we are thirsty, we can come to him.

So, let's sing the verse together, shall we?

Jesus said that if I **thirst**,
   I should come to Him.
   No one else can satisfy,
   I should come to Him.

For the Lord is good and faithful.
   He will keep us day and night.
   We can always run to Jesus.
   Jesus, strong and kind.

Weak

Jesus said. 'Come to me, all you who are weary and burdened, and I will give you rest. Take my yoke upon you and learn from me, for I am gentle and humble in heart, and you will find rest for your souls. For my yoke is easy and my burden is light.'

Matthew 11:28-30

Let's sing verse two of *Jesus, Strong and Kind.*

Jesus said, if I am weak,
I should come to Him.
No one else can be my strength,
I should come to Him.

For the Lord is good and faithful.
He will keep us day and night.
We can always run to Jesus.
Jesus, strong and kind.

Jesus was born in Bethlehem, but he grew up in Nazareth. Then, for a while, he lived in a village called Capernaum. It is on the west bank of a lake called the Sea of Galilee. It wasn't a big lake, and it didn't take long to sail across it—unless, of course, you got caught in a storm!

One day Jesus had gone across the Sea of Galilee with his disciples. On the other side he had rescued a man whose life had been made miserable by demons.

Then the disciples brought him back in their boat to Capernaum. The people on the shore could see them coming, and a huge crowd began to gather. Some of them had seen Jesus heal people who were sick. They wanted to see more!

The people in the crowd must have been asking all kinds of questions.

'Why did Jesus go to the other side of the lake? We don't really like the people over there!'

'Where exactly did he go? What was he doing there?'

As soon as Jesus stepped out of the boat he found himself surrounded by people. One was a woman. She looked frail, but nobody was paying her any attention.

Have you ever heard your mum say to someone, 'You're not looking well; you've lost your colour'? If your mum had seen this woman, that's what she would have said.

This woman was terribly ill. Then as she stood at the edge of the crowd something happened.

The crowd went quiet. People pushed forward to see what was going on. Those at the front of the crowd saw someone speaking to Jesus. Others at the back were asking who it was. Some people recognised him. It was Jairus, one of the leaders of the synagogue in Capernaum.

They all wondered why he had come to Jesus. What was he saying to him?

Can you imagine the crowd round Jesus? Maybe someone said, 'I can see him—yes, it is Jairus, but he's fallen down at Jesus' feet! He's holding him tight. He won't let go. He looks terrible. Something must be wrong!

'Jairus is telling Jesus that his little daughter is sick, really sick. He thinks she's dying. And she's only twelve! He's begging Jesus to come back with him and heal her. It looks as though Jesus is going! Yes, he is! Jairus has taken his arm. He's trying to hurry him along. The disciples are clearing a path for them through the crowd.'

If you'd been there you would probably have felt that the whole crowd began to move as one. Maybe you would have noticed that the sick woman was trying to keep up; but she was exhausted.

People were asking each other: 'Will Jesus get there in time before the girl dies? Will he heal her? What's going to happen?'

These were not the questions the sick woman was asking. Perhaps she was remembering the day, twelve years ago, when she heard that Jairus's wife had given birth to a little girl. Twelve years ago! That made her think. Twelve years ago – that was exactly the year she had started feeling unwell. She discovered one morning that she was bleeding from inside her body. Over time the bleeding made her weaker and weaker.

In those days they didn't have the wonderful hospitals we have today. This woman had tried to find a cure and had paid a lot of money for advice and medicine. However, no one had been able to help her. In fact she was getting worse, not better. Now all her savings were gone. Even if she heard about a doctor who might be able to cure her, she couldn't afford to pay him.

Then a thought came to her, there in the crowd.

Can you guess what it might have been?

She had heard that Jesus could heal people. If Jesus could heal Jairus's daughter who had only been alive for twelve years—might it be possible for him to heal a woman who had been ill for the same twelve years?

She needed to attract Jesus' attention, but it was impossible. She couldn't stop the crowd could she? Anyway, it wouldn't be right to stop Jesus when a little girl's life was at stake. That would be selfish! Then the sick woman had another thought, 'If I can get near enough to touch him—I think I might be cured. Even if I could just touch his robe I would be healed!'

She tried to push her way through to the front of the crowd. It wasn't easy. People don't like that, do they? Sometimes when it happens they say nasty things, and a fight breaks out. Somehow the sick lady made it. Now she was right behind Jesus! If she stretched out a little farther she would be able to reach him. So, she stretched out her hand, and she just managed to touch the hem of his garment!

Immediately, something seemed to happen inside her.

She felt better, and stronger.

She thought she might have been healed!

And she was.

However, just then Jesus stopped where he was, and the whole crowd stopped too.

Jesus must have needed all his strength to stop when the crowd was pressing around him. He had worked as a carpenter. So, carrying big planks of wood and all that lifting would have made him strong.

Jesus looked at the crowd. He knew somebody had touched him because he had felt healing power go out from him to someone else.

How did Jesus know that?

Some people can sense things, can't they? They can't always explain why. Sometimes you can sense things. You just know.

Jesus knew that someone had touched him. So, he looked at the crowd behind him and asked, 'Who touched me?'

The disciples were astonished at what Jesus said!

'Jesus! Of course someone touched you. Everybody's bumping into you, and touching you! You mustn't stop. Come on now; we've got to get to Jairus's house for the sake of his little girl. Please don't stop here!'

Can you imagine how Jairus must have felt? Every second counted. Why was Jesus wasting precious time asking the crowd who had touched him? There was no time to lose!

Jairus didn't know that by stopping, Jesus was helping him.

The woman came out of the crowd. She fell down at Jesus' feet, just exactly as Jairus had done!

She looked frightened; she was shaking.

What would you have felt like if you had been this woman? Do you think you would have felt embarrassed, or maybe ashamed?

Some of the people in the crowd knew her story. They knew that she had spent all her savings on doctors and medicines. Perhaps they thought she was stupid. 'She should have known that the medicines she bought would make her worse, not better!' People sometimes say cruel things, don't they?

Was Jesus cruel to her too? Why did he not let her go home quietly? Wouldn't that have been the kind thing to do?

Jairus must have hoped that Jesus wouldn't say anything to the woman. It might be too late for him to save his daughter.

However, Jairus had to wait and Jesus had to speak to the woman. It seemed cruel, but in fact, Jesus was being kind to both of them.

Jesus knew how desperate Jairus was. Yet, what he was doing would show Jairus that he really did have the strength to heal and to save.

So, why did Jesus talk to the woman?

He wanted her to understand that it wasn't his clothes that had the power to heal her. It was Jesus himself who had healed her!

The woman started telling Jesus all about herself!

'Jesus, I've been ill for the past twelve years.

I've spent all my money on cures that have just made me worse.

I didn't know what to do. I was desperate.

I heard that you could heal people.

When I saw you in the crowd going to Jairus's house, I knew I couldn't stop you. I thought if I could just touch you, I might be healed. And I did. I touched your robe. I feel healed!

I don't know what to say. I don't know if what I did was wrong. All I know is that I touched the edge of your robe and it feels as though all the terrible bleeding inside has stopped!'

Then Jesus said something that she never forgot.

The disciples didn't forget it either.

He called her 'daughter . . .'

She was probably older than Jesus, but he called her 'daughter.'

He told her that she didn't need to be afraid. He wanted to calm her down so that she would stop shaking. He was telling her, 'You are part of my family now. You don't need to be afraid. You believed that I was strong enough to heal you. I want you to know that I am also kind and I have brought you into God's family. You're his daughter now.'

However, Jesus said something else that was important for her to hear. 'You touched my robe, but it wasn't because you touched my robe that you were healed. It was because you trusted me. You believed I was strong enough to heal you and kind enough to help you. It wasn't touching me that led to your healing. It was trusting in me. So, now, go in peace. You've been healed.'

Jesus wasn't being cruel in calling the woman out of the crowd. He was being kind! He wanted her to understand that it wasn't his clothes that had healing power. No, it was Jesus who wore the clothes who had the power to heal!

However, the story doesn't end there. Of course not!

There is something else we all want to know about, isn't there?

We want to know what happened to Jairus's daughter.

Jairus must have felt that everything was going horribly wrong. While Jesus was still speaking to the woman who had been healed, some people arrived from Jairus's house.

'Jairus, we're sorry, but we've sad news. Your daughter has just died. Come home now with us. Jesus won't want to be bothered any longer.'

But Jesus is kind. The sick woman wasn't a bother to him, was she? Neither was Jairus.

The sick woman had been healed because she had trusted in Jesus. Jairus had heard what Jesus had said to her. He had seen Jesus' power at work. Would he trust him too?

Jesus then said to Jairus, 'You've just seen me heal this woman who came to me in fear and trembling. Now you're trembling and you're filled with fear. Jairus, you must do what this woman did: believe in me, trust me! You believed I was strong and kind enough to heal your daughter. Keep trusting me. Take me to your house; let's go to your daughter.'

Even though the crowd wanted to know what would happen next, Jesus did not allow them to come. However, by the time they got to Jairus' house another crowd had gathered.

In Jesus' day, when someone died, people wept and wailed loudly in the hope that they would be given money for showing how much they cared! That was what was happening when Jesus arrived at Jairus's house. It was a terrible noise.

Jesus told them all to be quiet! 'Jairus' daughter isn't dead,' he said, 'she's asleep.'

They all started laughing at Jesus and saying he was stupid and silly.

Can you imagine that?

They were laughing at Jesus who had healed a sick woman.

They were laughing at Jairus who believed that Jesus could save his daughter.

No wonder Jesus sent them all away.

What was he going to do?

Jesus took Jairus and his wife, as well as Peter, James and John, into the room where the little girl was lying.

Jairus was holding his wife's hand and putting his arm around her shoulder. Peter, James and John were standing against the wall. The room felt quiet and still.

Jesus went over to the little girl. He took her hand, and spoke two words to her in the local dialect, 'Talitha cumi!' (That means 'little lamb, get up').

And she did! She got up and started walking around—just the way you do when you wake up in the morning and get out of bed.

Can you imagine being in that room watching?

Jesus is standing there, smiling a little.

The twelve-year-old girl is walking around.

Mum and Dad are overcome with joy—what can they say?

Peter, James and John are looking at each other. They can hardly take in all that has happened in the last sixty minutes!

Then Jesus spoke: 'Friends, listen carefully. I told those people outside to leave. I said that your daughter is not dead, but asleep. And they laughed at us.

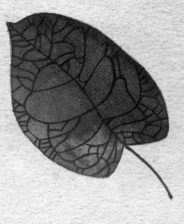

'Let them laugh. They can think whatever they want. They have turned against me because they do not believe in me as you do. So, I want you to keep to yourselves what you have seen me do in this room. You know what has happened. You have seen what I did. I know you trust me. That is all that matters. I must leave now. Your little girl is hungry! So, go and make her something nice to eat—something she really likes!'

Isn't it wonderful what Jesus did for the sick woman and for Jairus' daughter? Isn't it interesting that the number twelve—twelve years—is important in each of their stories? It's like two parts of the same story. Two people, one young and the other old, were in desperate need of help. Only Jesus could help them. And he did!

Jesus is still strong and kind today—for you and for me—when we trust him.

Don't the stories of Jesus with the very sick woman and the young girl make you want to sing about him again?

Jesus said, if I am weak,
I should come to Him.
No one else can be my strength,
I should come to Him.

For the Lord is good and faithful.
He will keep us day and night.
We can always run to Jesus.
Jesus, strong and kind.

Fear

Jesus said, 'Are not five sparrows sold for two pennies? And not one of them is forgotten by God. Why, even the hairs of your head are all numbered. Fear not; you are of more value than many sparrows.'

Luke 12:6–7

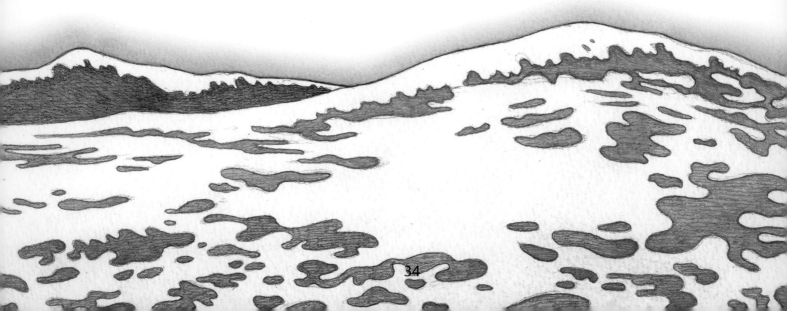

Let's sing the next verse of *Jesus, Strong and Kind*

Jesus said that if I fear,
I should come to Him.
No one else can be my shield.
I should come to Him.

For the Lord is good and faithful.
He will keep us day and night.
We can always run to Jesus.
Jesus, strong and kind.

Do you ever ask questions? I knew a little boy who was always full of questions, 'Dad, what is this?' 'Dad, why does this happen?' 'Dad, where are we going?' 'Dad, who is that?' 'Dad, when will we be there?' Questions, questions, and more questions!

Often, he didn't seem interested in my answers—he just wanted to know that there was an answer! Maybe you're like that too.

Here's a question to think about: Did Jesus ask questions when he was growing up?

We know from the Bible that the older Jesus got, the wiser he became. One of the ways you get wiser is by asking questions and thinking about the answers. Once, when Jesus visited the temple in Jerusalem, he asked the teachers there lots of questions. He even talked with them about the answers.

Later on, he asked different kinds of questions.

Sometimes, Jesus asked people questions even when he already knew the answers!

Is that strange? Not really. I am sure my mother must have asked me the same question a hundred times: 'Why are you so untidy?' But she already knew the answer! She wanted me to stop and think about why I was so untidy. Jesus was the same; he wanted people to think about the question and the answer.

One day Jesus asked his disciples a question and it was a difficult one for them to answer.

It all happened in a town called Capernaum which was beside the Sea of Galilee. Many of the people there were fishermen and had their own boats.

Two sets of brothers –James and John, and Andrew and Peter – lived and worked there. They had become disciples of Jesus and came from fishing families.

One evening, after he had been preaching to a crowd of people at the seashore, the Lord Jesus said to the disciples, 'Let's get into the boats and sail across to the other side.'

Now the Sea of Galilee is really just a lake. It is thirteen miles long and about seven miles across at its widest point. It's not really a big sea, is it? It usually didn't take too long to sail from one side to the other.

Jesus didn't tell his disciples why they were sailing across the Sea of Galilee, but they did what he asked since he was their Master and they wanted to please him.

36

However, something really frightening was about to happen.

When Peter was interviewed about his memories from this time, it was as if he could see in his mind all the details of that night on the Sea of Galilee. It was as though they were happening all over again inside his head.

'Yes, it was evening. Jesus had been preaching. He was tired. And when he got into the boat, he went to the wide part at the back and lay down! There was a cushion there. Before long, as the boat made its way across the lake, Jesus had gone to sleep!

'Then something frightening happened. The wind began to pick up. It got stronger . . . and stronger . . . and stronger. We had sailed right into a storm!'

Can you picture the disciples hurrying to take down the sails before they were blown over and capsized? The water is coming over the side of the boat. The disciples are trying to scoop it out, but it's coming in too fast. There's nothing they can do. If the wind doesn't die down, they'll sink. They won't be able to swim back to shore in this storm!

Are they all going to drown?

Is Jesus going to drown?

What is going to happen?

Everybody is panicking.

Everybody?

Well, no. Not everybody. Everybody *except one*.

Can you see what the Lord Jesus is doing?

It's amazing!

He's fast asleep in the middle of the storm!

Somebody needs to wake him up!

'Jesus! Wake up!'

'Jesus, help us! Please wake up!'

'We're drowning!'

'Jesus! Don't you care?'

What would Jesus have thought when he heard that question?

Wasn't that the unkindest thing they could ever have said to him?

Jesus knew they were in a panic; they were filled with fear. They weren't thinking straight. Even so, how could they say that he didn't really care?

Nobody had ever cared as much for them as Jesus did. Not even their mothers and fathers, brothers and sisters and friends cared for them as much as he did!

Maybe Jesus thought this:

'Dear panicking disciples, you don't know what you're saying. You have forgotten that the only reason I am here with you, and the only reason I came into the world, is because I care about you.

'I am with you because I love you.

'In fact, I love you so much that soon we will all go together to Jerusalem and I will be arrested and beaten up, and crucified there—all for your sakes.

'On that day, all your sins will be heaped upon me and I will become a sacrifice for you so that all your sins will be forgiven.

'All of that is going to happen to me because I care for you so much.

'Do I care about you? You have no idea how much I really care!'

However, before he spoke to the disciples – Jesus spoke to the wind and the waves.

He sounded like an army general giving orders to his troops in a battle—orders that everyone had to obey. Jesus told the storm to stop. He told the wind to calm down. He told the Sea of Galilee to become peaceful again—the way it had been earlier in the evening.

The wind stopped blowing. The Sea of Galilee became calm. And the disciples—what do you think they did?

They were in a state of shock.

They had been shocked by the storm.

They were shocked by what Jesus had done!

Were they seeing things?

Had Jesus actually stilled the storm—or was it all a bad dream, a terrifying nightmare?

No, it had really happened. Jesus had stilled the storm with a few words!

It was just then Jesus asked them the question, 'Why are you so afraid?'

And then he asked another question, 'Don't you trust me? Don't you have any faith in me?'

Why did Jesus speak to them like this? Was it cruel to ask them those questions when they were in a state of shock?

Sometimes when Jesus does wonderful things for us, we say to ourselves, 'This is so wonderful! Jesus is so amazing, I'll never forget it. I'll trust him in everything from now on!'

However, after a while, we just go back to the same old ways. We don't really trust Jesus any more than we used to do.

Jesus knew that might happen to his disciples. He knew he needed to help them right there and then! That's why he asked his question. It was important.

Jesus is sometimes like a surgeon—the kind of doctor who cuts into a patient's body. The surgeon needs to get inside the patient and fix whatever is making them sick. It's sore for the patient. Yet, it's the only way the surgeon can help them.

How is Jesus like a surgeon? He sometimes asked questions that hurt in order to get inside his disciples' hearts and minds. Jesus showed them their sin and failure. He needed to do this in order to heal them.

When Jesus asked his questions, 'Why are you afraid?' and, 'Have you no faith in me?' he already knew the answers.

They had forgotten who Jesus was, hadn't they?

They had forgotten that he was the King that God had promised to send—the King whose kingdom would have no end; the King who would bring peace.

They had already seen Jesus heal the sick and cast out demons. He had told the wind and the sea to be quiet and they had obeyed.

The disciples should have trusted Jesus even in the storm.

However, now they were whispering to each other, 'We thought we knew who Jesus was. Who is Jesus, really? We've still a lot to learn about trusting him!'

There is something really important for us to think about here.

Trusting and obeying the Lord Jesus doesn't mean that life will be 'plain sailing'! It doesn't mean that there won't be any storms. Sometimes life can get more difficult simply because you trust in Jesus. The disciples were just beginning to learn that.

What Jesus taught the disciples was this:

'In the storm you forgot that I was with you. You forgot that no matter what happens I am always with you. You forgot who I really am, didn't you? You even forgot that I am here with you in the world because I want to be your Saviour. You were so panicked by the storm that you completely forgot that even when I am asleep I am strong and kind. You've seen how strong I am. You know now that I came into the world to show you how kind I am. I want you never to forget that.

'Keep your eyes on me, and remember who I am. I'm not saying you'll never again be frightened. You will. But, remember how strong and kind I have been, then you'll not panic the way you did tonight.'

If one of the disciples had decided not to get into the boat with Jesus, would that have been a good thing? Well, he would never have been in the storm. He'd never have panicked. However, then he would never have seen how strong and kind Jesus was when the storm hit.

The disciples would face other storms in the future.

After Jesus died and rose again people would try to harm them and even kill them because they loved the Lord Jesus and wanted to tell others about him.

One time Simon Peter was arrested and thrown in prison. However, the night before he was due to be killed, God sent an angel to rescue him. What do you think Peter was doing when the angel found him? He was fast asleep. He was so fast asleep that the angel had to slap him on the side and tell him to wake up quickly!

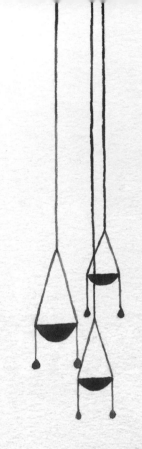

Does that remind you of someone?

Peter was now the one who was sleeping in the storm and needed to be wakened up! Peter had learned to trust Jesus.

He knew that he could trust him in any storm.

On the Sea of Galilee the Lord Jesus had saved him in the storm, and on the cross of Calvary he had died to save him from his sins. He knew that Jesus cared.

He knew that Jesus is strong and kind!

We know that too, don't we?

So, let's sing the third verse of *Jesus, Strong and Kind* again:

Jesus said that if I fear,
I should come to Him.
No one else can be my shield.
I should come to Him.

For the Lord is good and faithful.
He will keep us day and night.
We can always run to Jesus.
Jesus, strong and kind.

Lost

Jesus said, 'While I was with the disciples I kept them in your name, which you have given me. I have guarded them and not one of them has been lost.'

John 17:9

We've come to the last verse of *Jesus, Strong and Kind*. Are you ready to sing it?

Jesus said, if I am lost,
He will come to me.
And He showed me on that cross.
He will come to me.

For the Lord is good and faithful.
He will keep us day and night.
We can always run to Jesus.
Jesus, strong and kind.

Have you ever lost anything? If something important gets lost we want to find it again, don't we? Sometimes when we lose things it can upset us.

One day, long ago, my mum dropped her black purse in the snow. All her money was inside. When she hurried back to try to find it, the purse was nowhere to be seen. All the money for our food was gone. Can you imagine how she felt? It must have been awful.

One day Jesus said, 'I have come to seek and to save the lost.'

That's one of the most wonderful things he ever said.

When Jesus was on the earth many people wanted to be with him. Some of these people were tax collectors. Tax collectors work for the government.

In most countries people who earn money pay what's called 'income tax'. This is used to help run the country. It costs a lot of money for us to have all the things we are so used to having.

You might never have met a tax collector, but in Jesus' day everybody knew who the tax collectors were. They didn't like them. You see, Jesus' country had been taken over by the Romans. Roman soldiers marched down the streets and the government of the Roman Empire demanded taxes. After all, somebody had to pay for the army! Local people were appointed to collect the taxes. The government didn't care how much a tax collector charged, as long as the Roman Empire got the money it needed. So, some tax collectors charged the people a lot more than the Roman Government asked for. They could get rich quickly that way.

Everyone thought they were greedy cheats who made a lot of money.

This meant that tax collectors were lonely. Who would want to be a friend of a tax collector and invite him to dinner—or even be seen talking to him in the street? Only other tax collectors!

Yet, some tax collectors came to listen to Jesus. In fact, one day Jesus told a chief tax collector called Zacchaeus that he was going to come to his house! Imagine it—Jesus invited himself to the home of a tax collector!

Something wonderful happened to Zacchaeus that day. He became a disciple of the Lord Jesus. From the day he met Jesus he started giving half of what he owned to poor people. He also gave money back to people that he had cheated – and multiplied it by four!

However, there was a group of people called Pharisees.

They made extra laws for people to follow, laws that God hadn't given them. They did this in order to show that they were extra holy. Sadly, they didn't really love God. In fact, Jesus said they just loved themselves.

The Pharisees complained about Jesus and criticised him for being so kind to the tax collectors.

'Look at Jesus. He even eats with tax collectors! Jesus should keep away from tax collectors the same way we do.'

Another group of people were called 'sinners'. They also started coming to listen to Jesus and to talk to him about God. Everybody knew they had done wrong things. The Pharisees didn't like them and kept away from them. 'God doesn't love you,' they said. They were annoyed with Jesus for spending time with these people. They called them 'sinners' even although they were actually sinners themselves. We're all sinners, aren't we?

The Pharisees told the Lord Jesus not to go near those tax collectors!

'Avoid these sinners! They are all lost. Stay away from them!'

However, Jesus had come to seek and to save people who were lost! He would not do what the Pharisees wanted. So the Pharisees started criticising him!

'Look at Jesus—he welcomes these sinners. How can somebody who does that teach us about God?

'So, stay away from Jesus too!'

Jesus then told them a parable. Actually he told them three parables in one.

A parable is a story that has an important message.

A shepherd had one hundred sheep.

He probably counted them every night before he went to bed:
'One, two, three, four . . .' right up to one hundred.

Then one night he was counting . . . 'ninety-seven,
ninety-eight, ninety-nine, one hundr. . .' Where was number one
hundred? It was missing! One of his sheep was lost!

If he was counting his sheep at the end of the day it was probably
getting dark. Dark and dangerous. The shepherd made sure his
other ninety-nine sheep were safe, then he set out to find his one
lost sheep. He looked and looked for it until he found it.

Do you think the shepherd gave that sheep a good talking to?
After all, it had been dangerous for the shepherd to search for it.
Did he use his big shepherd's crook to give the stupid sheep a
few good whacks on the way home?

No. Here's what Jesus said, 'When the shepherd found his lost sheep, he lovingly lifted it up onto his shoulders and carried it all the way home. He happily sang a song of thanksgiving that he'd found his lost sheep! When he got back to his house, he called his friends and neighbours to come over. He was so happy that he'd found the lost sheep that he wanted them all to have a party with him!'

He loved the sheep that got lost; no wonder they had a celebration!

Then Jesus told a different story . . . a story about a woman who had ten coins.

That doesn't sound much. However, some coins are worth hundreds, even thousands of pounds or dollars! This lady's coins were quite valuable. They were certainly valuable to her.

One day she was counting them, 'One, two, three, four, five, six, seven, eight, nine . . . te . . . No!

'Where is coin number ten?'

She started again: '. . . one, two, three, four, five, six, seven, eight, nine, te . . . Oh no!' There were still only nine!

What would the woman do? She got a torch and went round the house, looking in every corner and crack to try to find coin number ten.

Then she squealed with delight, 'There it is! I see my coin! I've found my lost coin!'

She was so happy. She invited her friends and neighbours for a party.

Then Jesus had a third story to tell.

The third story was a longer one. The lost sheep was only lost for one night. The coin was only lost for one day. This story lasts for months and months.

It is a story about a man who
had two sons—a younger son
and an older son.

Brothers are sometimes different from each other, aren't they? That was true in this family. The older son always seemed to do the right thing. The younger son was always trying to catch up. As he got older he just wanted to get away from home so that he could do what he wanted. Why did he always need to be second? Why did he always need to be in his father's house following his rules?

The younger son decided to do something about it.

What he did wasn't nice. In fact it was horrible.

He went to his father and said something like this, 'Look, Father, when you die, some of your money is going to be mine. So, let me have it now, and then I can go and live my own life.'

That was almost like telling his dad, 'I wish you'd drop dead.'

His father gave the younger son what he asked for – although he probably had to sell some of his land in order to do it. Not long afterwards his younger son left home.

He went as far away as he could, into another country.

At last he felt he was free! He could spend his money any way he wanted. He could do whatever he wanted. He could please himself. And he did. He did exactly what he wanted to do.

He was careless and foolish. He ended up doing bad things. He spent every last bit of his money. He wasted it all.

Now he had to find a job. He had to take any work he could get, just to survive. All he could do was feed pigs! Imagine! Yuck!

He hated it. The pay was bad. All the people who pretended to be his friends when he had money quickly left him. As he fed the pigs he thought, 'These pigs get better care and better food than I do!'

Then, one day, something seemed to change inside him. He said to himself—

'I've been so stupid. I've done all these foolish and wrong things. Back home the people who work for my father have plenty to eat. Yet, I'm here, far away, and starving. Nobody cares about me—and I don't blame them. I'm not worth caring about!'

He was beginning to feel sorry for what he had done, and for the way he had hurt his father.

If he went home, what could he say to him?

The lost son started to practise a speech he could make, 'I'll go back home, and I'll say this: Father, I'm really sorry. What I did was wrong. I sinned against God. I know I hurt you. I am not fit to be your son anymore. Would you let me come home and give me a job?

I'll work as hard as I can for you—I promise. Please?'

So, he started on the journey back home. Somebody recognised him on the way and began to spread the news: 'Do you know the man with the big farm? Do you remember his younger son? The one who broke his father's heart? Well, I am almost certain I passed him on the road an hour ago. He looked a lot thinner than he used to be, but I'm sure that's who it was. He seemed to be going towards his father's farm. He's got a nerve coming home after what he did!'

Tired and hungry the son looked into the distance and noticed someone heading towards him. He seemed familiar. The man in the distance started running! Yes, running! It was his father! He had heard the news and was coming to see if it was true—was his son really coming home?

What would the father say?

Would he tell his ungrateful boy to get back to the pigs he had come from?

Would he tell him he never wanted to see him again?

No—the father's heart was full of love.

He threw his arms round his son. He held him tight. He still loved him.

The younger son started his little speech—the one he'd been rehearsing all the way home. 'Father, I've sinned against God. And I know I have hurt you. I'm not fit to be your son . . .'

However, his father was calling out to his workmen. 'Quickly, get some clean clothes for him; put one of my rings on his finger; get him a decent pair of shoes. Go back to the farmhouse and tell them we'll need plenty of meat to roast. I thought my son might be dead, but he's alive! He was lost, but now he's found. He's home! He's safe! No more work today! Tell everyone what's happened. Tell them how happy I am! We're going to have a party!'

What a great ending to the story!

Each of these stories is about finding something that was lost.

The shepherd went to find his lost sheep.

The woman searched to find her lost coin.

The father welcomed home his lost son.

The stories go from one lost sheep out of a hundred,

to one lost coin out of ten,

to one lost son out of two.

As the numbers go down from one hundred to ten to two, the value of what was lost gets bigger, doesn't it?

The lost coin was more valuable than the lost sheep.

The lost son was far more valuable than both the lost sheep and the lost coin put together!

And did you notice that all the stories end with a party!

Here's what Jesus said at the end of the first two stories. 'There will be more joy in heaven over one person who is sorry for the wrong things they have done and asks me for forgiveness, than there is over ninety-nine people who think they don't need forgiveness!'

There is always joy in heaven when someone turns to me and trusts me!'

Yet, sadly in the third story the party wasn't the end of the story.

There were two sons. So, what about the other son, the older brother? What happened to him?

When his father and younger brother arrived home, the older brother was working out in the fields. He thought he could hear a noise in the distance. It sounded as if people were laughing and dancing and having a great time. What was going on?

One of the farm-hands told him what had happened.

'Your brother has come home! Your father has arranged a party. I'm just on my way there now. You need to go back to the house quickly if you want something to eat and drink!'

What do you think the older brother did?

He muttered out loud that he wasn't going to the party.

He was extremely unhappy.

His father heard what had happened. He came out to find him. He begged him to join in the party, but the older brother turned on his father and said, 'Your son left home, took your money, and wasted it on his own selfish life. He did things that made you feel ashamed. Now he wanders back, and he gets a party!

'What about me? I've worked hard for you. I've never done anything wrong! When have I had a party? Never! You should be ashamed of yourself, welcoming your son when he shouldn't be allowed near the house! You should have sent him back to the pigsty where he belongs.

No, I am not coming to the party—not now and not ever!'

That must have hurt his loving father, don't you think? He had lost one son who had been found. Now it looked as though the older brother was the one who was lost.

The father was as loving to his older son as he'd been to the younger one. He said,

'Son, you've been at home with me all the time. You've had everything you could ever need. You know that everything I have is yours as well. But your brother—he was dead as far as we knew and now he's alive again! He was lost, and now he's found. He was in a far country and now he's home. We're not usually party people, are we? Only, there's never been a better reason for a party! We must have a party!'

Wouldn't it have been lovely if the older brother had said to his father:

'I shouldn't have said these things. You've been a great dad to me. You've always loved me. You've given me everything a son could ever want and you never stopped loving my brother. I'm glad he's home again. Of course we should have a party. My brother is safe, and he can have a new beginning. We can all have a new beginning!'

However, the older son said nothing. We don't know whether he ever came in from the fields to join the party.

Don't you wish Jesus had told us how the story ends?

Jesus must have had a reason for stopping there, don't you think?

Let's remember why Jesus told these three stories.

In the first story the shepherd stands for the Lord Jesus.

In the second story the woman stands for the Lord Jesus.

Then again, in the third story the father stands for the Lord Jesus.

The lost sheep, the lost coin and the lost son stand for the tax collectors and the sinful people who wanted to trust Jesus and were welcomed by him.

So, who does the older brother stand for?

He is just like the Pharisees, isn't he?

The Pharisees and the teachers of the law were criticising Jesus—just like the older brother.

At the end of the story, Jesus was showing the Pharisees and the teachers of the law what they were really like. They thought they were so much better than others, but if they

kept behaving like the older brother they would never celebrate Jesus' love and forgiveness.

The truth was, that like the older brother, they thought they were God's workers, not his children! They didn't really trust and love the Heavenly Father. They thought of him as somebody they worked for, not somebody they trusted and loved. They thought of other people as 'sinners', but didn't think of themselves that way. They didn't think they needed a Saviour.

So, Jesus ended his stories by showing the Pharisees and the teachers of the law the truth about themselves. They thought they were safe, but they were lost.

If they came to Jesus, then like the 'tax collectors and sinners', they too would be forgiven and welcomed home.

Eventually some Pharisees did. That's good news, isn't it?

Who else is Jesus speaking to in these stories?

Well, the Lord Jesus is speaking to us, isn't he? We're all different. We sin in different ways. We all sin and we all need forgiveness.

Jesus' stories tell us about his love for us, and how much he wants to find the lost, to bring us home, and to forgive us.

As we read on in the Gospel story we discover what the Lord Jesus did so that we might be forgiven.

Sometime after he had told these stories, Jesus died on a cross outside Jerusalem.

Sadly, lots of people in those days died that way. So, what was different about Jesus?

Unlike everyone else, Jesus didn't die because of his own sins, or because of anything wrong he had done. He died in our place to take the punishment we deserve for the wrong things we have done.

Three days later he rose again. That was a sign that his sacrifice for our sins had been accepted by God.

The Lord Jesus is now alive for evermore. We can come to him and even use the same words the younger son did: 'Lord Jesus, I have sinned against heaven and in your sight. I am not worthy to be yours.'

Jesus will do then, what the father in the story did. He will throw his arms around us, and forgive us, and welcome us into his home.

Jesus does that because he is strong and kind.

Like the loving father in this story, the Lord Jesus has come to us.

I wonder, have you come to Jesus? If not, you could do that when you're singing the song again.

So, let's sing the last verse of the song, shall we?

Jesus said, if I am lost,
He will come to me.
And He showed me on that cross.
He will come to me.

For the Lord is good and faithful.
He will keep us day and night.
We can always run to Jesus.
Jesus, strong and kind.

Jesus

We have come almost to the end of *Jesus, Strong and Kind*.

We've learned quite a lot about Jesus, haven't we?

First, we thought about the woman that Jesus met at Jacob's Well. Remember how he asked her for a drink of water? Then he explained to her why she was thirsty. He explained why she could never be satisfied unless she came to him.

Jesus said that if I thirst,

I should come to Him.

Then we thought about the older woman and the young girl who were both weak. The little girl even died. Jesus was strong and kind to them both. He healed the woman and he brought the young girl back to life.

Jesus said if I am weak,

I should come to Him.

After that we were sailing with the disciples on the Sea of Galilee and we learned how Jesus helps us when we are full of fear.

Jesus said that if I fear,

I should come to Him.

Jesus then told his marvellous stories about lost things. And we learned that because of our sin we are lost from God too—but Jesus came to die for our sins and to find us.

Jesus said if I am lost,

He will come to me.

That's why we can sing:

For the Lord is good and faithful.

He will keep us day and night.

We can always run to Jesus.

Jesus, strong and kind.

I hope you know you can always run to Jesus.

Have you ever done that and asked him to forgive you, and to be your Saviour, friend, and Lord? If not, perhaps you would like to do it now?

Let's sing *Jesus, Strong and Kind* one more time. And if you have never done it before, ask him to be your Saviour, your Friend, and your Lord

Jesus said that if I **thirst**,
I should come to Him.
No one else can satisfy,
I should come to Him.

For the Lord is good and faithful.
He will keep us day and night.
We can always run to Jesus.
Jesus, strong and kind.

Jesus said, if I am **weak**,
I should come to Him.
No one else can be my strength,
I should come to Him

For the Lord is good and faithful.
He will keep us day and night.
We can always run to Jesus.
Jesus, strong and kind.

Jesus said that if I fear,
I should come to Him.
No one else can be my shield.
I should come to Him.

For the Lord is good and faithful.
He will keep us day and night.
We can always run to Jesus.
Jesus, strong and kind.

Jesus said, if I am lost,
He will come to me.
And He showed me on that cross.
He will come to me.

For the Lord is good and faithful.
He will keep us day and night.
We can always run to Jesus.
Jesus, strong and kind.
Jesus, strong and kind.

Christian Focus Publications

Christian Focus Publications publishes books for adults and children under its four main imprints: Christian Focus, CF4K, Mentor and Christian Heritage. Our books reflect our conviction that God's Word is reliable and Jesus is the way to know him, and live for ever with him.

Our children's publication list covers pre-school to early teens. We also publish personal and family devotional titles, biographies and inspirational stories that children will love.

From pre-school board books to teenage apologetics, we have it covered!

Christian Focus Publications Ltd, Geanies House, Fearn, Ross-shire, IV20 1TW, Scotland, United Kingdom.

www.christianfocus.com

CHRISTIAN FOCUS PUBLICATIONS

| Christian Focus | Christian Heritage | CF4K | Mentor |

'What a beautiful combination of memorable music and meaningful truth from Scripture that will press the character of Jesus into the hearts and minds of children.'

Nancy Guthrie, author and Bible teacher

'In the vast expanse of our universe, there's no one more vital for us and our children to know than the Lord Jesus Christ. He is the mighty Creator of all and the compassionate Saviour who, in grace and truth, took on flesh to draw near to us. Why not take a moment to allow the grace and wisdom of Jesus to envelop your family, as eloquently taught by theologian and grandfather Sinclair Ferguson?'

Chris Larson, President and CEO, Ligonier Ministries, Orlando, Florida

'What Christian parent doesn't love to sing *Jesus, Strong and Kind* with their children? Now, thanks to Sinclair Ferguson, we have a great way to tell our children more about the Jesus they can always run to. Wonderful!'

Jonny Gibson, author, ***The Moon Is Always Round;***
professor of Old Testament, Westminster Theological Seminary, Philadelphia

'Every Christian parent hears the words of Jesus echo through their minds, "Let the little children come to me." We pray and hope that our children would indeed come to Him—that they would know Jesus in all His goodness, strength, and love. Here is a book to aid such a longing. With Colin Buchanan's song, *Jesus, Strong and Kind*, providing the framework, Dr. Ferguson takes readers on a biblical journey of encountering the beauty of this Savior. Each page reveals Jesus as the text of Scripture is unfolded before children's minds. But this is not simply a book for the mind; this is a book aimed at putting a song in every heart. Jesus is so very strong and kind. May our children know, love, serve, seek, desire, and delight in this Christ all the days of their lives.'

Jason Helopoulos, Senior Pastor, University Reformed Church, East Lansing, Michigan

'A thrilling combination of faithfulness and creativity, with questions that draw our children into the great story of the Bible. A model of the fact that to teach simply, you have to understand deeply.'

Rico Tice, author and Founder of Christianity Explored Ministries